T0190767

Clumsy Beauty

Clumsy Beauty

Poems for Hearing the
"I Love You" in Everything

J. K. Kennedy

MANDALA

SAN RAFAEL LOS ANGELES LONDON

CONTENTS

Author's Note

I have bad news. Nobody knows what they're doing. But I have good news, too! Nobody knows what they're doing.

This simple play on perspective illustrates how writing has helped me navigate a very beautiful, but often very messy, world. We have an almost unmanageable amount of information at our disposal these days. So much that sometimes it makes things even more confusing. So much that, most of the time, it's difficult to know what's true. Or even what's real.

Now, don't get me wrong, there's something wonderful about the "question everything" mentality, but where does it stop? Are we ever allowed to sit comfortably, be confident, escape that occasional hopelessness? These are the nagging tidbits that I love to struggle with and to nag back at. I see things almost daily that make me wonder, "Is my life on track?" "Am I behind?" "Should I be more productive?" "Am I a mess?"

You say, "Existential crisis?" I say, "Don't threaten me with a good time!"

About a year ago, during a particularly difficult stretch in my life, I decided that I was in need of a healthy habit. I settled on creative writing.

At the time, impeccably curated videos and ads on Instagram would have had me believing that I needed the perfect notebook, an aesthetically pleasing cup of cocoa, and a darling nook by a crackling fire in order to begin journaling . . . which, of course, I needed none of. (Aside from a new notebook. I always need a new notebook.)

I started with the goal of writing down at least one thought or emotion I was experiencing every day for six months. I also decided that posting these pieces online would keep me honest and accountable. So I opened up a new account and off I went into the scary and oftentimes judgmental world of social media.

The writing process was always enjoyable, but sometimes what I was writing was really gruesome. Hard to read. Even shameful. But regardless of the ick spewing out of me, people followed along. And not only that, but they commented, they understood, they even shared my work with others across multiple platforms. It was an unexpected and glaring delight when I realized I was allowed to embrace the feelings I had been cringing over just a few short months before. The revelation came from the catharsis I found in being able to share confidently.

I got to know myself on the page. One entry at a time, I was stumbling across myself. It was imperfect, too much information, messy, clumsy, beautiful. I watched as the tone of my work slowly began to change. Writing helped me reverse out of the dead end I'd found myself in. Suddenly, my voice and my messages started feeling a little more familiar. I heard myself over the other voices in my head for the first time in a long time. And I listened. And when you listen, without mangled pretenses, you start to hear the "I love you" in everything.

I noticed that most of the feedback I was getting was from folks just like me who were a little confused and maybe a little unsure, and sometimes that's really all we need. Some reassurance that we're all here together experiencing a *lot* of the same human stuff. When I gave myself the time to stumble into myself, I stumbled into you, too.

I hope these thoughts and poems help you see the clumsy beauty of it all and serve as a reminder that a little comfort and understanding may only be a scribble away.

—J. K. Kennedy

I. BEHOLD

I HAVE THE RECEIPTS

There are little receipts
showing up on my face.
    Lines, like on maps.
Proofs of purchase
    of a life well smiled at.
Grooves I hope I
begin to think of as
time's most ornate
passport stamps.

THE DESTINATION

It's near impossible to
feel lost
now that I know
    I am the path,
not just the traveler.
I'm the obstacle
and the advantage.
The descent and the incline.
But above all,
    the destination.

ITALIC LIFE

I'd like to live a more
italic life.
Delicately mindful of
what I emphasize.
Devoted only to that of importance.
A life that's
deliberately antithetical to the
inconsequential.

NAKED WONDERMENT

I think
jealousy is usually just
curiosity
cloaked in some
sinister desire,
and that's why I
do my best to
keep my wonderment
completely naked
at all times.

MORE THAN USUAL

Sometimes they are
more work,
but the days that are
    a little more than usual
are often my favorites.
When they love you . . .
When you tell me . . .
When I'm feeling . . .
When I notice . . .
    a little more than usual.

GEOMETRY

It's all geometry,
finding out
what fits.
It's not necessarily
good or bad,
it's just learning
what shapes and
whose shapes
belong
inside
yours.

From the Thought Pile

It's a good one to learn,
the sometimes impossible
art of zooming.
Knowing what situations to zoom in on
and which ones to zoom out from.
A new view can almost always
make this life a little
more comprehensible.

WATERCOLOR FEELINGS

You hate my
watercolor feelings
spilling this way and that,
catching every fiber as they plow on.
You'd rather I felt in some rich, fixed acrylic.
And one day, that will likely be the reason
I run.

From the Thought Pile

Somehow,
I still get suspiciously
  blissful
by way of small things,
and I think that means
  I'm doing great.

LOVE-ME-NOTS

Every day,
my whole universe
appears
on a daisy petal
that is next in line
to be plucked,
and a while back I decided
there are no more
love-me-nots.

POETRY

A lot of people think
poetry has to be
long or sad or about love,
but it can just be
how you smiled
  at yourself
   for yourself
in the mirror today.
Poetry is absolutely
that too.

DAISIES

I haven't met you, but
we're here together
sailing through space
on a ship that grows daisies
in some places,
and I think that should
mean a great deal more
to us.

WHAT'S HAPPENING

The world will have me

spending

so much time

worrying about

what's happening that

I forget

  I'm

    happening.

From the Thought Pile

I've been wasting
a lot of time in
yesterday and
tomorrow.
Sometimes I forget
   that it's always
      today.

MY FAVORITE BURGLARS

I watch lovingly as
daydreams
waddle by
with my
time.
The most adorable
little burglars.
I whisper,
"Help yourself, darlin,"
and sigh.

CATAPULTS

You won't believe how much
it can all change
(so fast)
    until it does.
Nobody tells you
that sometimes there are
    catapults hiding around
    nondescript corners.
Never forget that there is
always something
to be excited for that
you just don't know about yet.

From the Thought Pile

You look like
how a river sounds
when you're
not worrying.

I LOVE YOU IN EVERYTHING

You like to tell people
I'm strange,
but all I hear is
"I love you,"
because I know that's
what you mean.
And maybe that's what
makes me strange,
how I can always hear the
"I love you"
in everything.

TWO TOWNS

Honestly,
I don't know what's crazier,
believing everything happens
for a reason or
believing everything is
completely random.
Which is why I've set up camp
between the towns of
Chaos and Reason,
visiting each regularly
and paying tribute to the
balance and contrast
that each provides.

SLURRY OF MISCONCEPTIONS

I want to help you
see things differently.
I want to see your lips
come unstuck from
the straw you draw
your reality from.
You'll begin to laugh
when that slurry
of misconceptions spills out
then dribbles down your chin.
And I'll be there waiting to
wipe it away for you.

INVISIBLE GIANTS

What if we could see it,
the wind?
How awesome and terrifying
would that be?
And love, too.
I hope there would
be enough in the world
to sit back and marvel at.
Maybe it would look like
a sunset or lightning
coming down
    over
       us all.

From the Thought Pile

you think I
overcomplicate everything
I think I
decorate everything

EXPERIMENTS

When I was small,
I used to conduct
all sorts of messy experiments.
They usually involved
mud and maybe a
firefly or two.
Years later,
I'm working on achieving
that same level of wonder
and

    blatant disregard
      for results.

MASTER KEY

I am here and the person I am
because
a whole lot of people were
    kind and patient
with me,
and that
    very specific combination
is the master key
that lets a human unlock.

From the Thought Pile

I used to think
happiness was elusive,
but it isn't.
Most of the time,
it's just disguised as
something small.

SPOILS

Oh my goodness,
look at the confidence
on that one!
What must she be feeding it?
    The spoils of a lengthy
    internal war that's
      finally
        been
          won.

THE CATCH

I like to think
we all chose to come here
and we had a
specific reason for doing so.
The catch is,
we forget that reason
when we're born,
and whether we choose to
try to remember it
during this life
is an entirely
different decision.

MEMORIZING MOMENTS

I'm not saying
it's a test,
but you'd be crazy
not to study.
Life lies about the
importance of
The Final
and lives in the
moments
you'll wish you had
memorized.

From the Thought Pile

I get it.
Self-sabotaging
ensures that you
know how it ends.
And that makes things so
safe and predictable.
But what if the
unknown
is getting ready to embrace you?

HOUSEPLANTS

Easy to tell a real houseplant
from a fake one by
its imperfections.
You'll know real ones because
they might be dead or dying
in some spots.
I use this same litmus test on
humans.
You can usually spot the real ones
from their hurt parts.

CAPABLY EVER AFTER

Ours wasn't a love story.
A learning story, a growing story,
an end of story are all okay, too.
Work boots are more comfortable
than glass slippers.
And strong hearts are as worthy
as romantic ones.
I lived capably ever after and
embraced not needing more.

II. UNRAVEL

CLUMSY BEAUTY

It's hard work,
unfolding yourself,
that massive canopy
of consciousness
that you've kept
safely
tucked away.
It may take a lifetime to
tease out the wrinkles,
but there is no match for
its clumsy beauty,
an infinite bloom
bobbing on the wind.

DOUBT

Doubt is a
sneaky one.
It's always trying to
trick me
into thinking
I like windows
more than
doors.

From the Thought Pile

that addiction to
convenience
is what'll
have you
accepting the
immediate answer
over the
correct one

UNPACK

Your oaken anger is actually
a Russian stacking doll
of despair.
Unpack, my love,
lest you be just one forever.

MIND INVERSION

I need an inversion table

for my mind

so I can

dump out its

dark pockets

and watch as all my

half-chewed ideas and

wadded-up memories

  come tumbling out

    into the light.

OVERFLOW

I wonder if it ever stops,
the feeling that
I am constantly
putting things away,
cups, socks, feelings,
into cabinets, into drawers,
into secret spots
that catch the
overflow.

KNOCKING

Sometimes I have great big dam breaks.
When everything around me
is humming a little too high.
Maybe I let my to-do list
get one item too long.
It makes me wonder about
the people who
never go even a little crazy.
Maybe reality
eventually
stops knocking.
Or maybe they've learned not to listen.

I LOVE YOU

I think I say "I love you" too much.

It's strange how sometimes it

startles people.

But then I remember,

    that's why I'm here.

      To love and to startle.

MOSH PIT

I've let it get a little messy.
I've waved some feelings through
that I usually stop at the gate.
There are some deeply questionable
bits that are now bound to
bump into each other on the inside.
But who doesn't love a good mosh pit
every once in a while?

CERTAIN DANGER

I'm so much more comfortable in
the ambiguity of it all.
So happy to announce,
"I'm not sure."
I cherish the fluidity
that doubt allows
and find solace in the devil's advocacy.
To me, it's the certainty that may be
the danger.
It's the certainty that
will burn every single thing
outside of itself
without hesitation.

INSECURITIES

I think I'm done now
with this
mutant museum of
taxidermy insecurities
that I created and
tended to for so long.
They're all crooked mouths and
cattywampus eyes,
and I just don't want to
recognize them anymore.

PULP FANTASY

I'll always pick
the pulpy fantasy
over a
lukewarm reality.
Please, let me get
this life stuck in
my teeth before
I inevitably drown in
room-temperature time.

From the Thought Pile

Go on then,
  warn me.
Bang a fist,
I know you need to.
But I'm already
a thousand miles
away and as
unfit for caution
as I've ever been.

AUTOMATIC

If I'm not careful,
this life will make me
automatic.
I don't want to end up
as one big
reflex.
A scared, trembling
reaction.
So I'll hang on to
having a choice
in all matters for
as long as I am
strong enough to
keep making them.

HEIGHTS THAT WON'T KILL ME

I only fear heights that
won't kill me.
It's that prickly-pear,
all-or-nothing mentality
that's lodged in the
base of my skull.
No merciful moderation
for this
reality skydiver.

From the Thought Pile

Please, enough with the
preposterous positivity.
I'd like to feel angry or
sad until I am done without
also being waterboarded
by your relentless
ad campaign for
the bright side.

HUGS

I hug too hard.
Probably too long, too.
But after the recipient
waves past their initial
shock, I find that most
usually collapse in
to match my embrace.
So I guess this is
my side hustle now,
bringing back real hugs.
Because I think we need them.

INTRUSIVE THOUGHTS
ARE THE WORST

I always assume that
the worst thing about me
is way worse than
anyone else's worst thing.
I worry I don't even know
what my worst thing is, and
then I wonder who is
dying to let me know.
Actually, maybe
this
is the worst thing about me.

LIME

Sure, I'm a little bitter.
But bitter like
the taste of lime
when you weren't
expecting it.
Maybe a little shocking,
but somehow always
paired appropriately
with this world,
this reality, that isn't
always so sweet.

From the Thought Pile

it's okay
that they didn't expect you,
because, for a while there,
I bet you didn't expect
this you
either

DRASTIC MEASURES

I guess it's really just a
terror of my own making, as
I'm always ready to
roll the dice.
Perpetually on one foot from
pulling the rug out from
under myself.
I can't help flipping the table,
never in anger, only for satisfaction.
It seems I must always keep this
whirlpool swirling around me,
so I can't feel it
if I'm sinking.

LIAR

Your fear?
It's a liar.
That's why its story
keeps changing,
but yours
stays the same.

A FEW ANNOUNCEMENTS

I have
run out of
can-do attitude.
My thighs touch,
and they always will.
I am not accepting
any more
broken things at this time.
    Sometimes I need to
    make these small announcements
    to myself, for myself.
Because I am the one true
keeper of my sanity.

FACTORY SETTINGS

My best guess is that
they misread
the directions and
decided to make me
skeptical and hopeful.
It's certainly not bad,
but it's not easy,
and it's
magnificently confusing
most of the time.

From the Thought Pile

I am, of course, of nature,
so feel free to admire
my abundance,
but don't assume
I'm without
pits, thorns, or poison
for those seeking
to cut me down.

WHAT ARE YOU WHISPERING?

We all have little things
that we whisper to ourselves,
many times a day,
whether we realize it or not.
It's profound once you
start listening.
And then nothing short of
life-changing
when you finally decide to
swap out any cruelty
for kindnesses.

PURPLE PARTS

I skinned my knee a
couple months ago and it
still hasn't healed all the way.
Every time I look at the new
purple skin it reminds me
how silly it is that I expect my
exceedingly more complicated
parts to heal so fast.
I suspect I have more purple parts
than I am even aware of, and I'm
glad I don't have to wear
them on the outside while
they slowly mend.

PANIC

I wish I could lend some
of my Panic's confidence to
my capacity to be Calm.
Panic never knocks.
It has me pinned before
I even open the door.
Meanwhile, my Peace
paces in the alley around
the corner hoping
someone remembers it
said it was coming.

ON EXPECTING

I'm going to try to quit expecting.
I keep filling in blanks that were
never really blank to begin with.
Always racing to paint the future that specific
shade of dissatisfaction that I'm used to.
And with my expectations tightly
cuffed and locked away,
maybe I'll see the beautiful curious
things I've been vanishing
before they get a chance to be.

EXCUSES

I frequently obsess over the
exploration I'm not doing.
So I crouch in comfort
behind the woeful excuse that
the discovery of a thing is also,
so often, its ruin.

HUMIDITY AND A CAT

Humidity and a cat,
I've been
missing them both.
Air that hugs and
an aloof ghost detector
come October.
They feel like home.
They make me
remember somewhere
I wish was here.

III. REVEAL

MUST BE NICE

I wonder what it's like to
    hope cautiously.
I bet careful,
measured expectations
  must
    be nice.
Meanwhile, I'll be here,
tending to my
    (explosive) assumption that
everything is going to
turn out better
than I predicted.

DESTINY

I love a good coincidence.
For a moment I can
use my broadest brush
to paint over everything
in blush serendipity
and imagine that there's
a plan that's unraveling
just for me.

CASTING

Casting isn't just for spells,
it's for hope
and excitement
and sometimes even looks
and hooks, too.
Casting is for the net that you
meticulously braided,
the only thing strong enough
to hold your
wildest desires,
so do be careful where you
point it.

From the Thought Pile

How many things
are you keeping
under control
that were
only
    ever
       meant to be wild?

LILY PADS

It's the dream to
feel time more pleasantly.
Like lily pads.
Firm borders around clear thoughts.
Manicured feelings. Manageable.
Stepping stones for moments
   that don't
     run into each other.
Just one thing.
After another.

RELUCTANT LIGHTHOUSE

Oh, to be the reluctant lighthouse,
acknowledging my fragile willingness
to provide direction
to the ceaseless tide of dizzy explorers.
I'm not entirely sure when I assumed this post,
but I continue to be selected as the
low-functioning beacon that heralds in the lost.

COILED HOPE

I have that
go-go-gadget coiled hope.
The kind that is small
but then comes
clumsily tumbling out
when I
desperately need
something to grab on to.

From the Thought Pile

There's really nothing
I can do about it
once it gets going.
My excitement loves
to spill,
and I love to
let it.

PEOPLE FORAGER

I will forever be
foraging for
people who
help me see
the world in kaleidoscope.
The ones who notice
what I do not.
The ones who effortlessly
flip me upside down
so that I may come to
understand a beautiful view
that I did not even know existed.

From the Thought Pile

the problem was,
I'd been searching for fire
in florescent spaces

CURIOSITY

Sure, I want
lots of things,
casual, even frivolous,
with my desires.
No big deal.
It's when I get curious
about something,
that's when it's time to
buckle up.
That's when I know
I'm in trouble.

ESCAPE MYSELF

If I could just
  get out
    from under myself,
I would probably do
a strange little dance
and then go off in
some new direction.

INHIBITIONS

How many ideas
have we abandoned
because we imagined
someone laughing?
Exactly how much brilliance
is sitting along the side
of Inhibition Road?
Come, let's go collect the
bounty our egos
dared leave behind.

From the Thought Pile

I hope my fear

didn't go find

someone new

now that

I don't belong to

it anymore.

SPICY JOY

My favorite is the

spicy joy.

The kind that stays

hot in your chest.

A little reckless

consumption with

pink cheeks.

Good burn,

greasy

joy.

LITTLE TRIUMPH

What a triumph
a smile can be.
On your worst day,
one may float up
out of nowhere
unexpectedly,
and sometimes
that can
turn the tide
entirely.

CREATIVITY

There's nothing quite like
creativity leaving the body.
Like a scream, a squeal,
and a sigh all at once,
with all the precision of a
hundred hummingbirds
blazing toward one
empty heir waiting to
inherit.

PLENTY OF TIME

You can still
surprise yourself;
there's plenty of
time for
everything
you
stopped
expecting.

From the Thought Pile

Go find those
goose bumps.
Whatever makes
your skin
stand up
is worth
tracking down.

IT'S TRADITION

It's better to just
change traditions.
You don't always
have to make a
casserole, you know.
　　You can believe
　　you're beautiful
instead.
　　Bring that
　　to the party
instead.
　　It's tradition.

GAINING GRACE

I used to think that
grace just meant beauty,
something flimsy, even temporary.
But I've come to understand
that it's really an
extraordinary power.
It is the freedom from reaction.
And although I don't
possess it yet,
it has become something
I'm much more interested
in gaining.

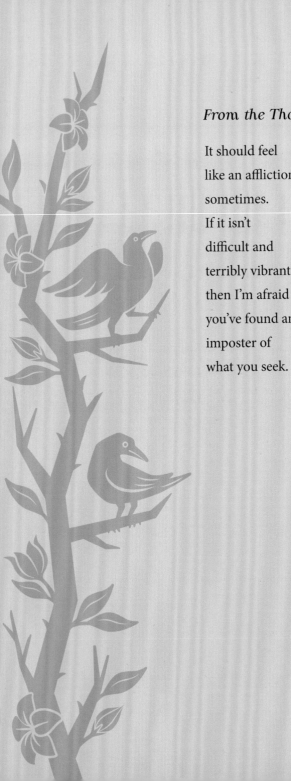

From the Thought Pile

It should feel
like an affliction,
sometimes.
If it isn't
difficult and
terribly vibrant,
then I'm afraid
you've found an
imposter of
what you seek.

MOMENTS OF CLARITY

I wish I knew where
the moments of
clarity come from.
They're like a friendly, fleeting
lobotomy,
or a satisfying sneeze for my
consciousness.
But inevitably,
the noise returns,
and I'm left
trying to find that
wonderful tickle
again.

LAST MEAL

I'm tired of taking
little hits of life.
Crumbs of aliveness
I find here and there.
I want the whole meal
all the time
because, after all,
it's my last one.

THE CHASE

Funny how when
you stop chasing
the wrong thing,
sometimes
the right thing
has time to
catch up with you.

From the Thought Pile

check in on your
willingness to receive
to make sure you
haven't accidentally
locked out
what's trying to
find you

WHAT I KNOW TO WANT WON'T DO

I don't know what I want,
and I'm no longer afraid
to admit that.
Because I think the
simple scope of
  "what I know to want" is
much too slim.
I think maybe
I want what I'm
  not even aware of
yet.

POWERFUL MOMENTS

There are powerful moments.
The ones that suck the
air out of your lungs so fast
you bend at the waist as if
your body was moved to
some involuntary prayer.
And sometimes you realize
later on it was a "thank you"
or an "I'm sorry" or a "why."
But these are all
prayers too, you see,
for the moments so enormous
they bow you down.

IV. AMPLIFY

LANDMARK WITH A LEAN

As hard as I may try,
I will never be able to
control what they think
of me. So I'll give up.
Or rather, I'll take down
all the busted scaffolding
I've built around me
that's holding up who
they'd rather I be.
Because I'd rather be a
landmark with a lean
than a franchisee.

I AM COMING THROUGH

"Please, just
get out of the way,"
I tell myself
as I skip over
yesterday's excuses
and take a
hard right past
a pile of doubt
that I don't remember
collecting.
    I   am   coming   through.

From the Thought Pile

No need to throw me
to the wolves;
I'm perfectly capable
of doing that myself.
I used to shy away
from those
hoping to cave me in,
but now I go
looking for them instead.

THE BAD STUFF, TOO

A lot of the time
I'm too stubborn
to see it,
but deep down I know
it's all an opportunity.
Everything.
Especially,
and fortunately,
the
bad stuff, too.

From the Thought Pile

I am growing
defiantly
up through the
cracks in the
concrete.
I am lifting
the ground
beneath me to
further open
the way
for others.

MISTAKES

The best part about
a mistake is
deciding if it will be
  an anchor
      or
        a sail.

VOLCANIC

Eventually you'll erupt,
and your borders will extend
in a slow, violent progression.
And sure, the waves will
break differently
around you now, but
at least this new
boundary is your own.

EASY, FELLA

Every few months I'll
go and try to
fix everything at once.
It's like a desperate
quarterly spasm
that doesn't end until
I remember that
I'm the one assigning
the due dates around here,
and I'm allowed
to be gentle in doing so.

BAD PRAYER

I used to say
"I'm sorry"
so much.
 Like, all the time.
I would apologize
just for being.
And then I realized
it was a
 bad prayer
that I was repeating over
and over.
I was telling this existence to
count me out.
And when I was finally
able to stop,
everything seemed to
start again.

WIN MYSELF OVER

I suppose that's probably
the point, though, right?
Realizing I'm here to
   win myself over.
Engage in some spirited
internal courtship.
It seems I have exactly
one lifetime to
lure myself

    in

      to

        love.

From the Thought Pile

I raised the price
on my
imperfections
when I realized
they are, in fact,
my value.

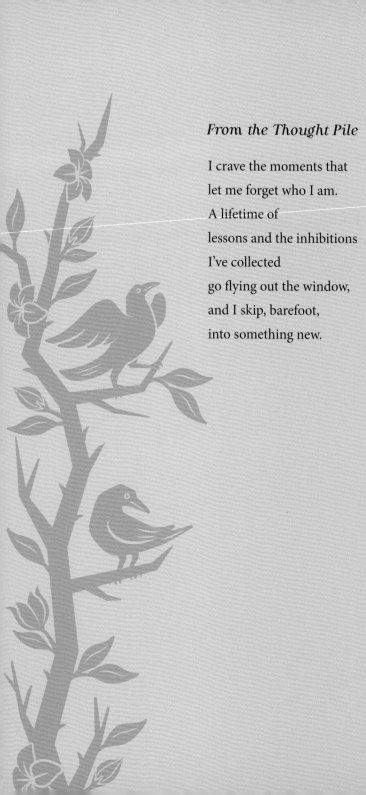

From the Thought Pile

I crave the moments that
let me forget who I am.
A lifetime of
lessons and the inhibitions
I've collected
go flying out the window,
and I skip, barefoot,
into something new.

SLOW DOWN

It's always a revelation
when I remember that
I can go slow.
When I'm rushing from one
thing to another,
my heart hikes up to
my throat.
Then I put my head back,
all the way back, exhale
and swallow it back
down to my chest.
     "Slow down," I say,
"where do you think you're going?"

N O

I wish I was brave enough
to use "no" as a
full sentence more often.
But I always have to
zhuzh it up
with some flowery explanations
and fake exclamations.
I wish I'd stop chipping away at
the solemn and singular
power of "no."

LITTLE BIG THINGS

I learn little big things
as I go. Like,
growth is almost always
uncomfortable.
Worry is a whoopee cushion.
Love is a giver and a taker.
And time is bent, so my life
was never meant to be a
straight line.
　The learning isn't always fun,
　but it sure does improve
　the living.

I HAVE COME LOOSE

I have felt it

coming

for a while now.

The ground

falling away from

my feet

and the mysterious

     lift.

I have waited for this.

     I   have   come   loose.

From the Thought Pile

There's a door
to a higher place
hidden just past
the commencement
of the things you're
afraid to do.
You're only ever
one step away
from a better next.

From the Thought Pile

my life has become
much less noisy
now that
my bold moments
have begun to
outnumber my
cautious ones

REFUSE TO NEGOTIATE

So frequently
and brazenly
the world tries to
talk me out of
being me.
Sometimes I wonder
why it doesn't have
anything better to do.
I hope a
victory bell rings
somewhere
every time I
refuse to negotiate.

THE MONSTER CALLED OPPORTUNITY

I've been hiding for a little while,

from the monster called Opportunity.

Because . . .

what if it doesn't

eat me up?

What if it doesn't

have a taste

for me?

So today I set out to do

just one scary thing,

and it left me feeling

quite delicious and

perfectly seasoned for that

monster called Opportunity.

From the Thought Pile

it's the

worst best

feeling

when you let go

of the reins

and realize your

grip on them

didn't matter much

to begin with

THE HANDSOME ASSASSINS

Comfort and Predictability
    are the two
        handsome assassins
that guard the door to
        what's next.

FEAR

I tried to keep my fear
at a safe distance
but, of course, it
followed me everywhere.
It wasn't until I let it
be near me
that I realized
it was just
trying to lead me out
from where
I came into it.

BELIEVING

There's a bit of bravery
in thinking about
new possibilities, isn't there?
    Because it takes believing.
And sometimes
believing can feel like
such a courageous thing.

THOUGHTS ON ANGELS

I think when they said,
"It was angels,"
they were talking about
thoughts.
Because they're the only things
that can appear
out of nowhere and
lift you
out of
just about anything.

From the Thought Pile

Here's to those
   who still
   wrap their
darkness
   (gently)
in light
   so as not to
   hide it entirely.

CAPTURE IT

If you're doing it right,
you're out here
    capturing life.
It's your extremely
exotic hostage
that's completely
unique to you.
You can keep it
in a photo or on a page
or even as a thought.
    But
        you must
            capture it.

Index of Poems

About the Author

J. K. Kennedy has been serving up bite-size poetry to a rapidly growing audience since October 2022. An accidental creative writer and incessant (over)thinker, she enjoys her quiet life in the country with her husband and two dogs. Her love of words comes from her beloved grandmother, who introduced her to the interdimensional art of storytelling. She also makes hearty greeting cards to help people express their love and gratitude for each other. This is her first book.

MANDALA

An imprint of MandalaEarth
PO Box 3088
San Rafael, CA 94912
www.MandalaEarth.com

Find us on Facebook: www.facebook.com/MandalaEarth

Publisher Raoul Goff
Associate Publisher Roger Shaw
Publishing Director Katie Killebrew
Editor Peter Adrian Behravesh
Assistant Editor Amanda Nelson
VP, Creative Director Chrissy Kwasnik
Art Director Ashley Quackenbush
VP Manufacturing Alix Nicholaeff
Senior Production Manager Joshua Smith
Senior Production Manager, Subsidiary Rights Lina s Palma-Temena

MandalaEarth would also like to thank Bob Cooper.

ISBN: 979-8-88762-111-1

Manufactured in China by Insight Editions
10 9 8 7 6 5 4 3 2 1

Insight Editions, in association with Roots of Peace, will plant two trees for each tree used in the
manufacturing of this book. Roots of Peace is an internationally renowned humanitarian organiza-
tion dedicated to eradicating land mines worldwide and converting war-torn lands into productive
farms and wildlife habitats. Roots of Peace will plant two million fruit and nut trees in Afghanistan
and provide farmers there with the skills and support necessary for sustainable land use.